THE ULTIMAT

GUIDE TO HAWAII FOR

2022, 2023, AND BEYOND

A Guidebook to this Beautiful State – Explore
Maui, Honolulu, Kauai, Lanai, Oahu, and more

RYAN JAMES

TABLE OF CONTENTS

INTRODUCTION

Hawaii is a beautiful Polynesian paradise located in the North Pacific Ocean off the west coast of the United States. And it is arguably one of the most beautiful states in the whole country. Tourists from all over the world flock to the island chains' sandy beaches, clear blue water, and breathtaking views. Formed from thousands of years of volcanic activity, the many islands of Hawaii offer endless thrills and activities for adventurous visitors while the serene beaches, tranquil waters, and peaceful resorts off the beaten path provide vacationers with ample opportunities to relax and unwind as well. There truly is not any place quite like the Hawaiian Islands.

So, are you finally ready to plan that dream vacation to Hawaii? Then you have undoubtedly noticed that Hawaii offers so many attractions and activities for tourists. And with so many fun adventures to be had, pristine natural wonders to explore, local cuisine to enjoy, and beaches to bathe on, it can be difficult to decide where to begin when it comes to planning that dream Hawaiian vacation.

The key to avoiding feeling so completely overwhelmed by the planning process is to focus on the types of activities you and your traveling companions would most enjoy. Consider who are you traveling with. (Hawaii is also the perfect place for solo travelers to visit). Are you taking your family to the islands and therefore you are on the hunt for family-friendly activities? Maybe you are planning your dream honeymoon or milestone anniversary and want a beautiful place to celebrate. Or maybe you are taking a friend's trip and want to explore the nightlife and local hot spots. Whomever you are traveling with, there are so many things you can find to do together that everyone will absolutely love. You just need to discover what type of group you are going to Hawaii with.

Are you an adventurous group who would enjoy zip-lining through tropical forests, rock climbing, or exploring underground caves? Is that crystal clear ocean water calling your name? If so, water activities like snorkeling, swimming with the dolphins, or Jet Skiing might sound fun to you. Would your group like to learn something new like surfing or sailing? Maybe you would like to take things up a notch and try your hand at more extreme water sports like scuba diving or deep-sea fishing.

Adventure and extreme water sports not your group's thing? There is no shortage of calmer activities to fill your time with. Hawaii is home to resorts with one-of-a-kind luxury spas and therapeutic treatments. And just because surfing and deep-sea fishing are a little more extreme for your tastes, that does not mean there are not a ton of more relaxing water-themed activities to take advantage of. You can casually float down small waterways on inner tubes, or slowly kayak through tropical rainforests, or maybe you would like to take a dip in a fresh Hawaiian Island spring. And do not forget about lounging on white-sand beaches or next to large stunning resort pools. While there, enjoy a tropical drink poolside or get a massage.

Is the group you are traveling with more into dancing clubs, bars, and exploring the nightlife? Maybe your group is not into all of the typical touristy stuff, and they want a more authentic Hawaiian experience? Or perhaps you find yourself in the position of planning a Hawaiian vacation with a group of people with a variety of different interests and desires? Well, the good news is that Hawaii offers something for everyone. Many somethings for that matter! So, there is no real need to stress!

In reality, there are hundreds, if not more, Hawaiian activities that could be listed here but instead, this guide will help you wade through the endless possibilities for your dream Hawaiian vacation and help you make some of those overwhelming decisions. Within this guide you will find key facts about the Hawaiian Islands, some travel dos and don'ts, and a detailed description of some of the most popular islands for tourists, so you can decide which islands best fit your personality and personal preferences. You will also learn about some of the unique attractions, must-try local foods, wild and marine life you might come across, and other valuable information needed when planning your trip.

So, sit back and let this handy travel guide make your vacation planning much, much simpler for you!

IMPORTANT
REFERENCE GUIDE

Throughout this travel guide, you will come across several activities and other facts that you may not be familiar with. So here is a quick reference guide for you to refer to if you find yourself needing help remembering what types of activities you might come across on the Hawaiian Islands.

Popular Hawaiian Activities That Will Be Referenced In This Guide

Bodysurfing— Bodysurfing is a more extreme water sport where you surf without any type of buoyancy device helping you stay afloat. Sometimes bodysurfers will put on a pair of adult swim fins in case they become tired while bodysurfing. Plus, these swim fins can help you catch waves or propel you forward easier.

Bodyboarding— Unlike bodysurfing, bodyboarding, also known as boogie boarding, does require the use of a surfboard. Bodyboarders will use the face, curl, or crest of a wave and ride it towards the shore. Then they will paddle back out, select another wave, and repeat the bodyboarding process.

Parasailing— Parasailing is a super fun activity if you are not afraid of heights. It combines the principles of kiting but in parasailing, you will be attached to the kite. The "kite," with you onboard, will be attached to a vehicle; in Hawaii, this vehicle is typically a boat of some kind, but cars or trucks could be used for land parasailing. Once the kite is attached, the driver of the vehicle takes off and the kite is pulled into the air by the speed of the boat and the wind. When the boat slows down or stops, you will slowly and safely descend back into the water.

Zip-Lining— Another activity not for those with a fear of heights but it is a fantastic activity for those who love a good adrenaline-pumping adventure, is zip-lining. With zip-lining, you strap yourself into a harness and zip down a wire or suspension line. The key to zip-lining is that the zip-line is suspended from a high place, like a mountain top, a tall building, through treetops, or the line could be suspended over a canyon, etc.

BASE Jumping— BASE jumping is when you attach a parachute to yourself and then jump from a tall place and use the parachute to slowly descend to the ground.

Snorkeling— Snorkeling is when you swim and explore the underwater world. This is allowed by using an eye mask and breathing tube. Often done in shallow waters, you must make sure the breathing tube stays above the water, so your breathing is not hindered.

Spelunking— Spelunking, also known as caving, is an activity where you explore natural caves and caverns. This past time requires flashlights and protective headgear at a minimum. For a more adventurous caving experience, you could need rock climbing gear to explore deeper caverns, but this is for a more experienced spelunker.

Windsurfing— A windsurfing board looks like a large flag is attached to a surfboard and this is not too far off from the truth. Windsurfing is a fun combination of sailing and surfing. Also known as sailboarding or boardsailing, you use the wind to propel you across the water. The wind fills your sail and pushes you on your board.

Fun Facts About The Hawaiian Islands

·❖———··———··———··———··❖❖❖———··———··———··———··❖·

Hawaii is actually made up of a chain of 137 individual islands. Not all of the 137 islands can be visited by tourists, and some are not inhabited at all. Each island was carved and grew right out of the Northern Pacific Ocean and formed into its unique landscape by volcanic activity. They started to form somewhere between 40 to 70 million years ago! These islands are home to different wildlife habitats and Hawaii is the only state in America to be home to tropical rainforests and is the only state in the union to grow coffee beans.

Have you heard of the island of Loihi? It is the newest island forming in the Hawaiian Island chain. This new baby island still has a few tens of thousands of years to go before it rises above the Pacific Ocean. It still has about 3,100 feet to reach the water's surface, but once it does it should be similar to Mauna Loa or Kilauea. So, do not plan on visiting this new island any time soon!

The state of Hawaii is made up of five counties and it has its own time zone, called Hawaii-Aleutian Standard Time. Hawaii also happens to be the widest state in all of America, going from east to west.

On August 21, 1959, Hawaii became the 50th state in America. That means there are generations of people living in the United States who were born before Hawaii ever became a part of the United States.

Hawaii is home to the world's largest telescope and boasts the honor of being home to more scientific observatories than anywhere else on the planet. Additionally, Hawaii also houses the world's largest wind turbine. The wind blades reach 400 feet.

Hawaii is the birthplace of surfing. That is right! One of the favorite water sports for people living on or visiting coastal regions was invented in Hawaii several hundred years ago and retains both societal and spiritual meaning for the people of Hawaii.

Each of the 137 Hawaiian Islands has its own distinct color and flower. For example, the island of Maui's official flower is Lokelani and its official color is pink. Each flower and color represent something special to each island.

Hawaii is absent of wildlife often found in the rest of the United States. For example, Hawaii does not have squirrels. They also do not have popular rodent pets like gerbils and hamsters, and it is in fact, illegal to bring these animals to the islands. And you may have heard that Hawaii does not have snakes. Well, for the most part, that is true; the islands do not have snakes, at least not snakes in the way that you think of them. But what Hawaii does have are these super tiny snake-like creatures that look more like worms. These are called Island Blind Snakes and again, these are extremely tiny and harmless. You are unlikely to see one but if you did come across Island Blind Snakes you would more than likely confuse it with a worm.

The state of Hawaii prides itself on being completely rabies-free. This means, among other things, that trying to travel or move to Hawaii with an animal or pet is extremely difficult. In fact, if you are hoping on bringing a furry friend with you to Hawaii, be prepared to go through several months of preparation, getting the right paperwork and certification, and do not forget about the quarantine process! So, unless your pet is a service animal you cannot live without, it is much simpler for you to plan on leaving your furry buddy behind.

Are you a major fan of casinos and gambling? Well, there is bad news on that front. Because while Hawaii offers an extreme abundance of activities and fun things to do, gambling is not one of them. In fact, Hawaii happens to be the only one of the states in America that have made all forms of gambling illegal. So, if gambling is your favorite pastime, you are going to be in for a disappointment when traveling to Hawaii.

The Hawaiian Islands have 50 State Parks, Two major National Parks, and seven other monuments and locations under the protection of the National Park Services.

They also have a uniquely Hawaiian postcard! Everyone loves a postcard, but the Hawaiian Islands offer a fun twist on this tradition. You can actually mail a coconut as a postcard. Some stores sell painted and decorative coconuts that are created just to be mailed back to the mainland United States as postcards.

Hawaiian is a beautiful language, but did you know that it only has 12 letters in the whole language? These are A, E, H, I, K, L, M, N, O, P, U, and W.

Each of the Hawaiian Islands was formed by at least one or more volcanoes. In fact, the island chain currently has six active volcanoes. Two of the most active volcanoes in the world are found in Hawai'i National Park on the Big Island; these are Kilauea which has seen close to 50 eruptions between 1912 and 2012, and there was another major eruption in 2018. Mauna Loa is the second active volcano in the park. And there are two other active volcanoes on The Big Island as well.

The Papahānaumokuākea Marine National Monument is one of the most interesting gems of the Hawaiian Islands. This monument is known to be larger than all of the other United States National Parks, combined! A linear cluster of pinnacles, atolls, cays with lagoons, submerged banks, and coral reefs, the Papahānaumokuākea Marine National Monument is the largest completely protected continuous conservation area in the whole country. Plus, the Papahānaumokuākea Marine National Monument is also the largest marine conservation area in the entire world, spanning a distance of nearly 1, 243 miles.

President George W. Bush established the Papahānaumokuākea Marine National Monument as a UNESCO World Heritage site in 2006. Then several years later, President Barack Obama expanded the size of the monument to include a larger perimeter into the ocean. Making it the world's largest protected marine conversation area.

Bonus Fact: Papahānaumokuākea Marine National Monument is now more than double the size of the state of Texas, but its geographical location makes it difficult to receive many visitors.

Basic And Bonus Fun Facts About the Hawaiian Islands

Hawaii has its own state motto; in the native Hawaiian it reads Ua Mau Ke Ea o ka 'Āina i ka Pono, which is translated into English as "The life/the sovereignty of the land is perpetuated in righteousness."

The Hawaiian state bird is the Nene. Nenes are often referred to as the Hawaiian goose. They are found on the islands of Oahu, Maui, Kaua'i, Molokai, and Hawai'i (also known as the Big Island).

Hawaii's state tree is the Candlenut tree.

Hawaii has an official state mammal is known as the Hawaiian Monk Seal, while Hawaii's state fish is the Reef Triggerfish and the state reptile is the Gold Dust Gecko.

The state flower of Hawaii is the Yellow Hibiscus.

Obviously, the state dance of Hawaii is the Hula.

Their state gem is the black coral.

The capital of Hawaii is Honolulu, and it is located on the island of Oahu.

DOS AND DON'TS
OF TRAVELING TO
AND FROM HAWAII

Traveling to Hawaii is not like traveling to other states in America. There are several things to consider when planning your trip and other cultural behaviors to observe once arriving. There are a host of items you cannot bring into the state or leave with. For Americans, traveling to Hawaii has some similar restrictions as traveling abroad. Except for American citizens, you will not need a passport to fly in and out of the state; visitors from other countries will still need their appropriate travel documents.

But no matter where you are traveling from, planning a Hawaiian vacation comes with a good deal of prep and likely a long flight or two. Leaving California alone is a 10-hour flight. You would not want to put the time and effort into getting to Hawaii, only to be denied entrance because of something silly.

Check this quick guide on what you need when planning your trip and what to do when you finally arrive.

Packing

Even though Hawaii is a part of the United States, the islands have specific rules about what is allowed in. For example:

1. Certain fruits and vegetables are a no-no. All fruits, vegetables, and other agricultural products must be inspected before being brought into the state and while many of these agricultural items will be allowed in after inspection and the proper paperwork is filled out (Yes, there are forms you must fill out before you can bring in fruit.), there are still certain items that will not be allowed into

Hawaii without going through quarantine and certification processes. These include but are not limited to:

♦ Pineapples—Pineapples are major exports from Hawaii and the state does not want to risk letting any diseased or compromised pineapples into the state.

♦ Corn on the cob

♦ Coconut

♦ Passion fruit or seeds

♦ Radishes

♦ Turnips

♦ Horseradish

♦ Daikon

♦ Other cruciferous vegetables

♦ Citrus or fruits with pulp from places like Puerto Rico and Florida

♦ Bamboo

♦ Sugarcane

♦ Coffee plants or seeds

♦ Palm Plants

2. Pets will have an extremely hard time getting into Hawaii. The state of Hawaii will not risk diseases like rabies getting into the state. They pride themselves on being a rabies-free state so

trying to bring a furry friend to Hawaii will require a lot of preparation, more paperwork, and a quarantine process. So, unless your fluffy buddy is a guide animal, it is better to find a trusted friend or family member to leave your pet with while visiting Hawaii.

3. Other animals are not allowed to be brought into Hawaii by tourists under any circumstances. These include snakes, Hawaii is a snake-free state and if a couple of snakes got loose, they would quickly breed out of control. They could cause some serious damage to Hawaii's natural ecosystem. For this reason, other animals like hamsters, gerbils, and squirrels are also not permitted in the state of Hawaii.

4. Avoid the bulky beach, sand, and other water toys. While it may be tempting to look at the photos of those beautiful white sandy beaches that Hawaii has to offer and think that you will need to bring sand toys to keep those kiddos entertained while visiting the beach, in reality, these items are a major hassle to try to fit into your suitcase, and once they get wet and covered in sand, are you really going to try to bring them back with you? There are plenty of

places to get cheap throw-away beach toys in Hawaii if you think you will genuinely need them, which you likely will not. Save time packing and save room in your suitcase for better items. Leave those plastic toys at home.

What Are the Items You Should Bring With You to Hawaii?

Now that you understand what you cannot bring into the state of Hawaii, here is a quick list of items you absolutely should bring with you. Keep in mind, that Hawaii is extremely tourist-friendly, and if you forget your shampoo or phone charger, you would have no trouble getting these items while on the island. But Hawaii itself is a little pricey and these items might have a fairly high mark-up on them.

1. Comfy walking shoes— no matter what type of activities you are planning on doing while in Hawaii, you can probably bank on doing a great deal of walking. So, packing shoes that are both comfortable and supportive will be vital.
2. Sunglasses— Hawaii is known for its beautiful sunny weather and you will absolutely need a good pair, or two, of sunglasses handy.
3. Sunscreen— It is Hawaii! You are not going to want to spend a ton of time indoors, so you can

count on getting more than your fair share of the sun! Bring sunscreen to prevent a nasty sunburn that would ruin the rest of the vacation.

4. Chargers and batteries— remember to pack the charger for your phone, laptops, video games, tablets, iPads, etc. and if you happen to bring electrical devices that require batteries, be sure to pack enough batteries to help get you through your trip. If you do forget these items, it is not the end of the world and you should be able to find a store that carries what you need, but it might take a while and you do not want to blow part of your vacationing budget on a charger. Plus, you are likely looking at a 10-plus hour-long flight, and you would hate it if your phone or other electronic devices' batteries were to run out, and then you would have no way to charge them in the air.

5. Personal toiletries— Hawaii is different than any other place you have visited before and if there are specific toiletries and personal hygiene products you simply cannot live without, then it is best to ensure you do not leave them behind. It could be difficult to locate your specific brand of shampoo or specialty

toothpaste. And again, if you can find them, they will more than likely cost more in Hawaii than at home.

6. Flip Flops or sandals— while comfortable walking shoes or tennis shoes are a must for most outdoor activities, they may not be the best choice for frolicking along the beach. You can avoid tracking half of the beach back to your hotel room by choosing to wear a comfortable pair of flip flops or sandals when hanging out or walking to and from the sandy beach.

7. Prescriptions or other necessary medical equipment— if you have a daily prescription or need a special medical device, like a sleep apnea machine, it is better to remember those items when packing. There is nothing more frustrating than being in Hawaii and discovering you left your medication back at home.

8. Beach and swimming attire— do not forget to pack your favorite bathing suit or suits! You will want to enjoy Hawaii's beaches and the fancy resort pools while on vacation. So, it would be a real bummer for you if you could not find a swimsuit or beach attire that fits or is

within your budget while in Hawaii. It is always a good idea to bring your swimming clothes with you. Better safe than sorry.

9. Your personal identification——you will not be allowed to board the plane without your legal state identification or other forms of valid I.D. Be sure to grab it before heading to the airport. Note, that American citizens will not need to bring their passports as Hawaii is a part of the United States. But if you are traveling from anywhere else in the world you will need your passport and/ or other legal travel documents to get into the state of Hawaii.

Behavior

While Hawaii is technically a part of the United States, up until the late 1950s, Hawaii was its own country, with a rich history and culture. So, that is why in some respects it may feel like traveling to a different country when you visit Hawaii. With this in mind, here are a few local behavioral and cultural norms you should observe when visiting the Hawaiian Islands.

For example, when it comes to driving on the islands, it is best to ditch those big-city road rage issues. Drivers in Hawaii are more relaxed and in less of a hurry than the drivers in most of the rest of the United

States. If you rent a car while visiting Hawaii, be prepared to drive slower and more casually than you are used to. Hawaiians do not rush and are huge believers in island time. So, do not crowd other drivers or honk your horn, and leave those less than friendly hand gestures back on the mainland. And with an average speed limit of 55 miles per hour on the highway or less, you can expect to get pulled over and receive a hefty ticket if you speed. Out-of-state driver money can be extremely appealing to local Hawaiian officials.

That laid-back attitude is not only reserved for driving in Hawaii. So, you can expect that service in places like bars, restaurants, and other service industries might take a little longer than you might be used to. But that is okay, you are on vacation in a tropical island paradise after all, what is your rush?

Another important thing to remember when visiting the Hawaiian Islands is that these islands are home to proud Pacific Islanders with strong cultural ties to the islands and there are some sacred locations you will be visiting. Be respectful! You would hate it if thousands of tourists came to your hometown and disrespected it. So, when visiting Hawaii, be mindful of your surroundings, and follow any signs or guidelines you see when touring the islands.

Speaking of being respectful, leave the natural habitat the way you found it. Avoid taking sand, rocks, shells, coral, and other natural elements. Removing items from beaches, forests, and National Parks could not only be illegal but is also extremely disrespectful to locals and the island. There is even a local legend about the goddess Pele, where if you remove sand or lava rock from the Big Island you will be cursed with bad luck. And the only way to remove that bad luck is to return the sand or lava back to the island. Also, it is super illegal to take anything from a National Park and many of the beaches on the Hawaiian Islands.

When exploring the Hawaiian beaches and snorkeling in the ocean waters, keep in mind how valuable and fragile some of the underwater habitats are. This is especially true for coral reefs. The coral reefs are already under attack from climate change and pollution so do not do anything to make things worse. This means, hands-off. You can observe but do not touch and do not break pieces of the coral off the reef. If you want coral to take home, buy some from a pet or exotic fishing store. Leave the coral reef itself alone.

While you are not taking anything from the Hawaiian landscape, focus on not leaving anything behind, as well. This means, do not litter! You must remember to be respectful of the land and the natural habitats. So, put your trash in the proper trash bins and do not harass, feed, or bug the wild and marine life. Take all the photos and videos of those cute animals and stunning marine life you would like but do not interact with them. Just let them be!

Free those toes! Being respectful of the outdoors and nature is great but do not forget about respecting the indoor homes of the locals as well. In Hawaii, it is customary to remove your shoes before entering someone's home. So, if you get an invite into a local's home, be prepared to remove those shoes!

Pay attention to the signs. While exploring the Hawaiian Islands you will see signs telling you where you can and cannot go, and other signs will be visible with safety information. Some of the signs that are directing you away from dangerous areas, and remember there are active volcanoes on a few of the islands, wildlife fires, and rock slides can also happen. And other locations are off-limits to visitors because they are sacred. So, follow the signs to stay safe and avoid offending, or getting a major fine, while visiting Hawaii.

Be kind and respectful to the locals. Hawaii is a major tourist attraction, and many locals are friendly and make their living in the tourist trade. But other locals may not always be super excited to deal with hundreds of strangers around them all the time. But how would you feel if you were in their shoes? So, you can show respect to locals by being polite, not speeding or honking your horn when driving, cleaning up after yourself, and treating the natural lands properly.

Speaking the Language

Hawaii today is home to several different cultures and a wide variety of people call Hawaii home. Not to mention the large variety of people who flock to Hawaii for vacation each year from all around the world. So, it might not be uncommon for you to come across people speaking different languages. However, you can expect most if not all major tourist locations, resorts, and restaurants to have staff who speak American English. This means you should have no trouble communicating when you need to.

But what is so interesting is that Hawaii is the only state in the country that has two designated native languages. These are Hawaiian and English. So, you can expect to run into many people speaking in their native Hawaiian language during your visit.

So, be sure to keep in mind that overall, speaking English throughout your trip is perfectly fine. But learning a few Hawaiian words or phrases is also polite. But what is considered unacceptable and outright offensive most of the time, is when tourists or non-locals try speaking Pidgin. Pidgin is a native language spoken through the Islands by the locals and many Native Hawaiians would prefer it if visitors did not try to speak Pidgin. Think of it as culturally insensitive.

Leaving

When it comes to saying goodbye to the Hawaiian Islands, which is probably the hardest thing you will have to do on your trip, there are a few things to keep in mind. This is mostly related to what you can and cannot take with you back home. Like with entering Hawaii, there are certain fruits, vegetables, and other plant life that you cannot take into the mainland of the United States. There are also several protected species and other naturally occurring elements in Hawaii that you cannot take with you at all or that have a specific limit to how much you can leave with, sands and volcanic rock for example. Hawaii is dedicated to protecting its natural habitats and the beauty of the islands, so with this goal in mind, they cannot allow tourists and other visitors to take all of their valuable resources from the islands. Here are some examples of what you can and cannot take with you when leaving Hawaii.

- ◆ Lava Rock from a National Park—there are National Parks in Hawaii with active volcanoes where you can see and maybe even pick up some lava rock. But be sure you put that rock back when you are done examining it. It is illegal to remove items from a National Park and this includes the lava rocks.

Plus, there is a native Hawaiian legend about taking lava rock from the Big Island of Hawaii. As the legend goes, the goddess Pele gets extremely upset when people remove her lava rock or sand from the island. So, anyone who takes a piece of lava rock will be sent bad luck from the goddess. The only way to reverse this bad luck is to return the lava rock or sand. In fact, if you cannot fly back to Hawaii's Big Island to return the rock or sand yourself but you still want to reverse your bad luck, there is an official mailing address that you can ship these items back to:

Hawaii Volcanoes National Park
P. O. Box 52
Hawaii National Park, HI 96718- 0052

But it is probably better to not risk the goddesses Pele's anger, or other legal actions, in the first place. Leave lava rock and sand you find on the Big Island where you found it.

- Sand—While the TSA will technically allow sand in both your carry-on and checked bag, the state of Hawaii has some specific rules about taking sand off their beaches. So, unless otherwise noted at the beach you are visiting, consider the action of taking sand from a Hawaiian Beach illegal. In fact, depending on the amount of sand you try to take and which beach you take it from, you can expect to pay a fine of up to $100,000 for stealing sand. So, yeah, it is probably just better to leave that sand behind. They probably sell sand at the gift shops anyway.
- Certain fruits, vegetables, and other plant life cannot be taken from the Hawaiian Islands back to the mainland of the United States, including:
- Fresh fruits and vegetables, with some exceptions that will be listed below
  - Berries including:

- o Fresh coffee berries
- o Sea Grapes
- ◆ Cactus plants
- ◆ Cactus plant parts
- ◆ Cotton or cotton bolls
- ◆ Fresh flowers of the jade vine
- ◆ Mauna Loa
- ◆ Kikania
- ◆ Fresh pandanus
- ◆ Live insects or snails
- ◆ Seeds with fruit clinging
- ◆ Fresh seed pods
- ◆ Soil
- ◆ Or any plants in the soil
- ◆ Sugarcane
- ◆ Swamp cabbage
- ◆ Mock orange
- ◆ Coral, whether fresh from the reef or bleached coral fund on the beach.

On the other hand, here are some agricultural and natural items you can bring from Hawaii back home:

- ◆ Coconuts
- ◆ Coffee

- Great news for coffee lovers, people are allowed to bring back unlimited amounts of roasted or unroasted coffee or green coffee beans. Without having to deal with any restrictions.
- Commercially canned or processed foods
  - This includes both processed fruits and vegetables
- Dried seeds
- Decorative arrangements
- Fresh flowers, like,
  - Leis
  - Foliage, with the exceptions of any citrus or citrus-related flowers, leaves, or other plant parts, as well as
  - Jade vine or Mauna Loa also are not allowed into the mainland United States from Hawaii
- Hinahina, also known as. Spanish moss
- Fresh pineapple- yummy, yummy!
- Irish and white potatoes
- Treated fruit, such as
  - Papayas
  - Abius
  - Atemoyas

- Bananas
- Curry leaves
- Dragon fruits
- Lychees
- Longans
- Mangosteens
- Starfruit
- Rambutans
- Sweet potatoes

*Note: these fruits will need to be treated at a USDA-approved facility. Then packed into sealed boxes that are properly marked and stamped.

- Seashells
  - Not land snail shells!
- Seed leis and seed jewelry
- Wood, this includes driftwood and sticks
- Wood roses that are dried

THE MOST POPULAR HAWAIIAN ISLANDS FOR TOURISTS TO VISIT

Hawaii may have 137 islands but not all of these are open to visitors or tourist-friendly. Actually, not all of these islands are even inhabited. But there is a handful of Hawaiian Islands that are extremely welcoming to tourists and here are four of the top islands you might consider adding to your list for your dream Hawaiian vacation.

The Big Island, Also Known As The Island of Hawaii

Officially titled the Island of Hawaii, but often better known as the Big Island, is the largest island in the state of Hawaii. Actually, it is almost twice the size of any of the other Hawaiian Islands. It is a relatively new island, all things considered. And this island is still growing! Each day, the Big Island grows a little bigger. Home to the Kilauea volcano, located in Hawaii's Volcanoes National Park, it has been adding to the island landmass. Kilauea is an active volcano that pumps an endless and continuous flow of lava that frequently increases the size of the Big Island's southeast coastline. Over 570 acres have been added to the island since the early 1980s. When Kilauea erupted back in May 2018, this one eruption increased the landmass by 857 acres.

The Island of Hawaii is large enough that it would likely be extremely beneficial for you to rent a car or some other form of transportation during your stay. While several islands in Hawaii are small enough to walk around or use a bike as the main source of transportation, the Big Island simply is not one of them.

The size of the Big Island is only one aspect that attracts visitors here. With unparalleled geological features and an impressively diverse atmosphere, the Big Island is a major tourist attraction.

Speaking of atmosphere, did you know that the Big Island is home to 10 of the world's 14 climate zones? That means one moment you can be exploring the Polar Tundra on top of snow-covered mountains one day and then take a hike through the Tropical Rainforest or visit the desert the next day.

These different climates will have some temperature variations, but you can expect pretty pleasant weather all year long. In fact, at sea level, the average temperature is somewhere around 85 degrees during the warmest parts of the summer months. And in the winter, the temperature usually hangs out around the 78 degrees mark. So, it is basically swimming weather and summer attire any time you choose to visit.

Where to Eat

What is the point of taking a dream vacation to Hawaii and not eating a bunch of yummy, local cuisine? Enjoy some of the freshest locally grown ingredients prepared by world-class chefs! Some of the must-try restaurants on the Big Island include:

Merriman's Hawaiian Restaurant tops the list of the many best places to eat on Hawaii's Big Island. There are several Merriman restaurants throughout the Hawaiian Islands but if you find yourself on the Big Island, this is a must-stop to curb your hunger. This restaurant is the perfect place if you are looking for a fancy, dress-up night out! They use local and fresh ingredients, and you will not soon forget the taste of the unique Hawaiian dishes they offer.

Manta Restaurant is a great place to fill up and get the day started. This restaurant is known for its amazing and delicious breakfast buffet. Meaning that Manta Restaurant is a good location to fuel up so you can be ready for a full day of exploring. The buffet is loaded with local flavors, fresh seasonal fruits, and Hawaiian sweet treats!

Da Poke Shack is the place you should stop by for lunch. Famous for their seafood and poke, Da Poke Shack gets you ready to head back out for more Hawaiian fun. But be sure to get to Da Poke Shack early because they are only open until they sell out each day.

Things-To-Do

Unsurprisingly, the largest island in Hawaii is not lacking in fun activities and adventurous exploration opportunities. So, let's start with the beaches!

The Big Island is not only home to some of the most beautiful beaches Hawaii has to offer, but it also has a variety of types to select from. One part of the island is made up of those picturesque white sand beaches Hawaii is famous for, and other parts have black sand beaches! And yet, there are still beaches that offer even more variety when it comes to sand coloration. Some of these beaches are perfect for relaxing and sunbathing, others are more naturally rugged and ready to be explored, and others offer visitors the opportunity to be even more active. From suffering to snorkeling and getting up close and personal with some of Hawaii's famous underwater marine life, you could spend your whole vacation on the beaches of the Big Island and still not see and do everything offered by these sandy paradises.

A few of these stand-out beaches include the four-mile-long **Carlsmith Beach Park**, famous for calmer waters and sea turtles! **Onekahakaha Beach Park**, also located in Hilo Bay, provides warm and shallow waters. These waters are also known to be so clear that you see right to the bottom of the bay. The calm shallow water is perfect for visitors wanting a relaxing place to swim or snorkel.

For something a little different, hop over to **Punaluu Black Sand Beach**, located south of the Hawai'i Volcanoes National Park. Punaluu is home to that famous black sand. The volcanic activity on the island is what turns that sand black. The beach itself is outlined with palm trees growing coconuts and if you are lucky, you will get a peek at Hawaii's infamous green sea turtles resting on the black sandy beach. Note, that you cannot touch or interact with turtles or take any of the black sand off the beach or back home with you. Remember, both the turtles and the sand are protected.

And while you are exploring the beaches on the Big Island, be sure to add Pohoiki Beach to your list. This is the Island of Hawaii's newest black sand beach. How new? Well, this black sand beach did not even exist prior to 2018. In 2018, Kilauea erupted leading to the creation of this beach. Swimming is allowed here as there is a lifeguard on duty and you can surf here, but surfing is only recommended for expert surfers because the water can get a little rough.

While exploring the stunningly beautiful beaches on the Big Island, be sure to try your hand at a few of the island's water activities. Snorkeling and surfing are great activities to try but there are a plethora of other things to try here as well. These activities include scuba diving and swimming with stingrays at night! Other water sports you can try on the Big Island include parasailing, kayaking, and body surfing.

Moving more inland, the Island of Hawaii offers many fun things to do on land as well. Take a bike or horseback ride through forests, past breathtaking waterfalls, and volcanic landscapes. You can also hike or casually stroll through Hawaii Volcanoes National Park. Or consider touring a coffee farm.

If you need to give your tired feet a break, there are several great options for guided tours on the island. These do include more traditional bus tours of course. But if you want something a little different, there are guided taxi and limo tours you can try out as well.

Golf lovers rejoice as the Big Island is home to several world-class golf courses. Some courses are designed for golfers of all different skill levels and interests. And to be honest, how many other golf courses in the United States come with the view and nearly perfect weather conditions of Hawaii?

So far, we have covered water activities and land activities, but do not forget about the air! The Big Island hosts several amazing options for you to explore the unique Hawaiian Island and stunning landscape from a helicopter or fixed-wing aerial tour.

So, does the Big Island of Hawaii sound like the perfect destination for you? Then be sure to pack comfy walking shoes and lots of sunscreen!

Maui

Probably one of the best well-known of the Hawaiian Islands is Maui. Maui, also sometimes referred to as The Valley Isle, is Hawaii's second-largest island. Also home to some truly beautiful beaches, Maui is well known for whale watching. The migrating humpback whales can be seen during the winter months of December through April, although Humpback and other whales may still be spotted throughout the rest of the year as well.

Maui is such a stunning and is such an amazing place to visit that for more than 20 years the island has been named the best of all the islands in the United States, according to Condé Nast Traveler.

Want to know what makes Maui so unique amongst the Hawaiian Islands? Maui is actually three different islands, not just one. And these islands get to boast of being the home to the tallest seaside cliffs in the world. Are you brave enough to walk up and look over the edge? Be careful!

While exploring all that Maui has to offer, you can take a break and cool off under the iconic and ancient **Banyan Tree**. This Banyan Tree is one of the largest trees in the entire United States and it is a must-see when traveling to Maui. You can also enjoy a real and traditional luau while in Maui, with all the traditional music, foods, and dancing you have come to associate with Hawaiian culture.

Where to Eat

Maui is world-renowned for their farm to table restaurants and for using some of the freshest ingredients you have ever eaten. So, when in Maui, eat as Mauis do! Home to world-famous chefs, some of whom have competed on cooking shows like *Top Chef* and *Iron Chef*, Maui is the perfect destination for foodies around the world.

MonkeyPod is not just a fun name, MonkeyPod is one amazing, must-try restaurant. Named after the trees that grow throughout the Hawaiian Islands. Pop into MonkeyPod to listen to live music and fill up on their delicious and vast menu items. Known for their shrimp and mushroom potstickers, wood-fire pizzas, poke tacos, corn chowder made from fresh local coconut milk and lemongrass, and much more!

Sam Sato's is a small diner located in Wailuku and you will want to arrive early because there is always a line of people waiting to order a loco moco, chow fun, dry mein, banana hotcakes, and other tasty noodle dishes. Sam Sato's is only open for breakfast and lunch, so this is a daytime restaurant only.

Ululani's Hawaiian Shave Ice is a great place to stop for a refreshing and sweet treat. With more flavors and varieties than you could possibly try, Ululani's Hawaiian Shave Ice is the best way to cool and down relax after a busy morning of exploring Maui.

Things-To-Do

Come for the yummy local food options and beautiful landscape and stay for all the fun you can stand! On Maui, there is no reason anyone would get bored. Unless, of course, the idea of relaxing on a beach all day sounds like the perfect vacation for you! But if you are looking for more fun and adventure, check out these cool activities to fill your time.

Maui boasts some of the most popular and unique beaches in Hawaii. 120 miles of coastline circle the island and it has over 30 miles of accessible beaches. Each year visitors flock to swim, play, and explore the warm waters off Maui's coast. With white, black, and even red sand beaches to choose from, it is not difficult to see why Maui's beaches are so popular with tourists. The beaches of Maui are broken up into the three main regions of Maui's Island: North Shore Maui Beaches, West Maui Beaches, and South Maui Beaches.

Some of the must-see beaches that Maui has to offer include:

Makena Beach State Park, also known as the Big Beach. Makena Beach State Park is located in South Beach Maui and is one of the most popular beaches in all of the Hawaiian Islands. Relax on this beautiful white beach or enjoy snorkeling, swimming, or even fishing in the clear blue ocean waters. As an added perk, Makena Beach State Park has a lifeguard or two on duty for added safety.

D.T. Fleming Beach Park is so amazing that it was named the best beach in the United States. The official title was America's Best Beach in 2006. Located in West Maui, D.T. Fleming Beach Park is best known for both bodysurfing and bodyboarding. While beautiful, D.T. Flemings Beach Park's waters can become dangerous with heavy surf and strong, unpredictable rip tides. So, the bottom line is to be mindful of water conditions before entering.

Waianapanapa State Park Beach, located on the North Shore of Maui Beach, is known for its stunning black sand. It is a popular beach for campers and is great for people who love to snorkel. Plus, it offers several freshwater pools to explore.

While exploring the many beaches that the island of Maui has to offer be sure to try your hand at **surfing**. The surfing conditions on most Maui beaches are fantastic. Never been surfing before? Do not worry, several beaches have surfing instructors and you can take lessons!

While you could spend your whole vacation relaxing, playing, and swimming on Maui's beaches, there are dozens of other fun activities you could also enjoy on the island.

For example, one heart-pumping adventure you might be interested in is **biking down the side of a volcano**. Hop on a rented bike and ride down a 37-mile track, down the slopes of a real volcano. You will get to enjoy the natural beauty and stunning landscape that Maui has to offer as you descend the mountainside.

Keep the volcanic-themed fun going by snorkeling through a volcanic cone. Home to just one of the three volcanic atolls in the world, **Maui's Molokini Crater** will offer you a unique snorkeling experience that you literally cannot get anywhere else.

If you happen to be more of a history buff who loves learning about ancient cultures, Maui has something special to offer you as well. On Maui, you can explore parts of the islands that are more secluded and you will see signs of the people who lived there thousands and thousands of years ago. One of the main draws here is **Ki'i Pohaku petroglyphs**, images that depict a large range of shapes and forms. You will be able to view these petroglyphs near Kaiolohia on Shipwreck Beach and al Kaunolu, and along the Polihua Trail.

Interested in getting off your tired feet but still want to explore? One of the main attractions in Maui is **the 50-mile one-lane Road to Hana Highway.** This road twists and turns through dense untamed forests. Discover stunning waterfalls and untouched streams. Pack a picnic and your hiking shoes so you can get out and explore the natural wonders along this iconic road. You may also want to bring your swimsuit along as there are natural pools you can go for a swim in.

So, how does swimming with sharks sound to you? A little too adventurous maybe? Well, the good news is that you can stay both safe and dry by visiting the **Maui Ocean Center**, which is the largest aquarium in all of Hawaii. Here you can view the marine life found in the local Pacific Ocean and beyond. View and learn about tropical fish and colorful sea corals, and do not forget about the amazing sea turtles! Then get ready to get up close and personal with the sharks! Do not worry, again this is a safe and dry activity. The Maui Ocean Center has an underwater passage that you can walk through and view sharks and other sea life as they swim overhead and all around you. This is a 7,50,000-gallon shark tank that you will be walking through as the tiger, white tip, and gray sharks swim all around you.

Kauai

The island of Kauai, also known as the Garden Island, is mostly covered by Tropical Rainforests. A large portion of its coastline is outlined in breathtaking cliffs and pinnacles, while other parts of the island are surrounded by beaches and long stretches of coconut trees. Overall, Kauai is known for its stunning beauty and natural landscapes. Kauai has gorgeous waterfalls, mountains, forking rivers, deep emerald valleys and forests, and several other natural wonders that make the Hawaiian Island such a dream paradise.

Kauai is Hawaii's fourth largest and oldest island. It is also the northernmost island in Hawaii's chain. Parts of Kauai cannot be reached by foot or vehicle and instead require a form of air or sea transportation in order to access them. Other parts of the island are home to small villages and are an amazing representation of the culture and traditions that Hawaii has to offer.

Where to Eat

Opakapaka Grill and Bar is a fresh seafood restaurant located right by the ocean on Kauai's North Shore. If you love seafood, Opakapaka Grill and Bar has a wide variety of seafood offerings including fish tacos and drinks like the Ha'ene Mai Tai. Their menu also includes non-seafood options including large burgers, wings, and pasta. They boast the title of being the last place to grab a bite before you reach the Na Pali Coast.

Pink's Creamery is a dairy lover's paradise. If you happen to be Lactose Intolerant this might not be the restaurant for you. But if not, pop by to try some Pink's Creamery shakes, Smoothies, and other creamy, icy treats. If you are looking to supplement your sweets with some tasty food, Pink's Creamery also serves Hawaiian grilled cheese, in three local flavors, from the hours 11:00 a.m. to 6:00 p.m.

Fresh Bite Kauai is a great place to stop by for lunch. Their hours are 11:00 a.m. to 3:00 p.m., Friday, Saturday, Sunday, and Monday. They are closed Tuesday through Thursday. Fresh Bite Kauai is a food truck that uses fresh and local fruits and vegetables in its dishes. Their menu contains salads, quinoa, wraps, sandwiches, poi, and hand-cut French fries.

Things-To-Do

Kauai features a truly one-of-a-kind beach known as **Eleele**. While the other islands have beautiful white sand beaches, stunning black sand beaches, and still other beaches have red or yellow sand beaches, the island of Kauai has a glass beach. Along with white sand beaches. This unique beachfront is considered a little off the beaten path, but it is well worth the extra effort to get there. Just do not plan to walk barefoot on this beach! The ground of this beach is made up of round pieces of smooth glass. This colorful glass is spread out over the top of the basalt rocks. Unfortunately, while the glass beach is unique, it is not natural. Years of glass building up in the ocean and washing up on shore are what make up the glass beach. Broken bottles and glass items shatter and the jagged edges have become smooth over time due to exposure to natural conditions and elements. Then over time, the waves carried these glass pieces to this beach in Kauai.

If you are looking for a fun and unique Hawaiian adventure, then look no further than **mountain tubing**. While visiting Kauai, hop on an inner tube and float downstream around a mountain.

The Blue Room is a cave that glows and is located on the northern coast of Kauai. It is an otherworldly experience to go through this cave. The real name is Waikapalae Cave. The cave is home to a blue hue grotto and appears to glow almost magically. In order to reach The Blue Room, you will hike past two other caves along the trail; while these are impressive caves in their own right, they pale in comparison to what The Blue Room has to offer. The blue waters in the glowing cave are amazing but do not dive in. There is no natural filtration system within these waters and the risk of harmful germs is extremely high. You do not want the water to enter your body and open cuts or sores are at especially high risk. And no matter what you do, do not drink the water from this pool!

For a more peaceful experience, visit **The Himalayan Academy**. The Himalayan Academy is the closest thing to the experience of being in Nepal, Tibet, that you will get in the United States. Except this version is located in a lush tropical forest and not in the rugged terrain in Nepal. At The Himalayan Academy, Polynesian and eastern regions, and western ways of life all come together. This is an outreach and educational center for the Hindi religion and the academy practices the teachings of ancient gurus from parts of India. This place of worship combines ancient teachings and traditions with modern technology.

Visit the **Allerton Garden** if you are on the hunt for one of the most beautiful spots on Kauai. This 89-acre garden has been referred to as the Garden of Eden, it is that stunning. You will find the Allerton Garden located in the Lawai Valley on the southern coast of the island. The Lawai Stream weaves through the gardens adding to the area's natural beauty.

OAHU

The island of Oahu is rich in history and is one of the most popular islands for tourists to visit. Oahu is home to Hawaii's capital, Honolulu, Waikiki, and it is the island where the Pearl Harbor attack took place. Sometimes referred to as The Gathering Place, Oahu is the third largest island in the Hawaiian chain but the most populated overall. This island is also home to a large and diverse population with inhabitants with both Eastern and Western roots calling the island home. The island has a lot of vacation attractions as well, and it combines all the beauty and charm of the other islands with the laid-back island mindset while hosting big city living in regions of the island.

Oahu certainly is not lacking in places to explore and fun activities to fill your time. There are also some major resorts on the islands with beautiful pools and lounging areas for those who want to relax. The island hosts gourmet restaurants and local eateries that are sure to impress even the pickiest palate.

If you are looking for a hot nightlife scene, then Oahu is the island for you. The best clubs and bars are located in Oahu. Dance the night away in Waikiki, then the next day get ready for more bar hopping fun. While here, grab some local craft beer in Honolulu and enjoy some of the best shopping options the island chain has to offer.

Sometimes referred to as the surfing capital of the world, Oahu is also the island you head to enjoy some fun and more extreme water sports. The beaches in Oahu beckon world-class surfers and novices alike.

Where to Eat

Helena's Hawaiian Food is located in the capital of Honolulu and features unique Hawaiian dishes. The food is amazing, but the hours are a little limited to Tuesdays through Fridays from the hours of 10:00 a.m.

to 7:30 p.m. Some key menu items include Kalua Pig, Pipikalua Style Short Ribs, Lomi Salmon, Haupia, and Luau Squid.

Giovanni's Shrimp Truck is a food truck style eatery that sells some creative and tasty shrimp-themed dishes. Shrimp scampi, the "No Refunds" hot and spicy shrimp, and Lemon butter shrimp to name a few. They also offer other non-shrimp options if you are not a huge seafood fan. For example, they offer the Jumbo Garlic Hotdog and Homemade Mac Salad. This casual eatery is a perfect stop for lunch or for grabbing a bite on the go.

Leonard's Bakery is a great option to indulge your sweet tooth. Try some Portuguese and Malasadas donuts, sweetbreads, pastries, and other various sweet treats, like cookies, pies, and muffins. Try something savory like their ham and cheese and Portuguese Sausage Wraps. Opened in 1952, Leonards' Bakery is a staple in Honolulu.

Things-To-Do

The **Pineapple Garden Maze** is a giant maze located on the Dole Pineapple Plantation. It is in the shape of, you guessed it, a giant pineapple. The Pineapple Garden Maze has the distinction of being the largest plant-based maze in the world. The maze covers two acres and there are more than two and a half miles of walking paths through the maze. With dozens of ends, paths that lead to nowhere, and others designed to confuse you, this is a life-sized puzzle to keep you busy for a while. But do not worry too much, there are multiple pathways going to multiple exits, so you will not find yourself stuck in the maze forever! The maze features over 14,000 plants, so you will be able to enjoy the beauty and sweet scents while traveling through the maze. Take your time and enjoy the maze or rush through quickly and earn a spot of recognition for being one of the fastest people to make it through the maze. However, the average person takes an hour or so to solve the maze.

While visiting the Dole Pineapple Plantation be sure to check out their other attractions including a fun train tour and enjoy some tasty fresh pineapple while there.

Oahu and Honolulu specifically have some amazing g nightclubs and bars to explore if you are more of a night owl. Put a few of these on your list:

Duke's Waikiki, located next to the ocean, is known as the barefoot bar. They are famous for the mixed drinks and cocktails and have a great late-night bar menu. But this bar is only open until Midnight, so be sure Duke's is an early stop on your night out.

The **Tchin Tchin!** The bar is a wine bar located in Chinatown. If you are not a major wine drinker, no worries, they do have a large menu of mixed drinks, cocktails, and craft beers. On the top floor with an open roof, have your drinks while enjoying the refreshing island breeze.

SKY Waikiki is the place to go if you are looking for a more classic nightclub. Located on the 19th floor in a Waikiki high rise, SKY has some truly breathtaking views of Honolulu. Being a more traditional club, they have a dress code, offer bottle service, have a VIP section and they are open until 2:00 a.m., so you can dance the night away!

Kelley O'Neil's is a real Irish Pub in the middle of Honolulu. Open from 11:00 a.m. to a whopping 4:00 a.m. every day they have traditional Irish drinks, including Guinness of course! They offer live music from 5:00 p.m. to 3:30 a.m. every night if you feel like dancing.

If you are looking for more of an adrenaline rush, then try zip lining through the Oahu rainforests. There is no shortage of zip line options on the island of Oahu. For example, Kualoa Ranch offers its **Jurassic Valley**

Zipline experience. Take a zip line tour through the Ka'a'awa Valley, where there are seven tandem zip-lining tours, five hiking trails, and two suspended bridges to explore.

If you are more of a history buff, the island of Oahu is the place for you. **Pearl Harbor** is located on Oahu; you can spend the day entrenched in the history of that fateful day. You can visit the Battleship Missouri or the USS Arizona Memorial, or you can simply walk around the city exploring. You can tour the Battleship Missouri every day from 8:00 a.m. to 4:00 p.m. from Tuesday through Saturday. While at Pearl Harbor be sure to stop by the Pearl Harbor Aviation Museum and go climb aboard the USS Bowfin Submarine Museum and Park or the USS Arizona.

While on the island of Oahu be sure to learn a little about the Polynesian people by visiting the local **Polynesian Cultural Center**. Part living museum and part of what is described as a cultural theme park, the cultural center is a one-of-a-kind place unique to the island of Oahu.

Other Exciting and Fun Things To Do and Explore on the Hawaiian Islands

⸰⸱━━━⸱⸱━━⸱⸱━━⸱⸱━━⸱⸱━━⸱⸱━━❖❖❖━━⸱⸱━━⸱⸱━━⸱⸱━━⸱⸱━━⸱⸱━⸱⸱

State and National Parks

The Hawaiian Islands are home to 50 State Parks, two large National Parks, and seven other National Park Services protected areas or monuments. These public lands are protected and it is illegal to remove anything from the natural habitat in these parks. But the lands within these parks' boundaries are stunningly beautiful and well worth exploring. Each park offers something different but here are a few standouts to explore.

Hawai'i Volcanoes National Park—this park is located on the Island of Hawai'i, otherwise known as The Big Island. This National Park is truly unique because, among other geological wonders, the park encircles two extremely active volcanoes. In fact, it is not uncommon for parts of the park to close for small periods of time due to volcanic activity and active fires. Mauna Loa and Kilauea are two of the most volcanically active volcanoes on the planet today, and it is widely believed that Kilauea itself is currently the most active volcano. Mauna Loa and Kilauea are so active that there is a decent chance you will be able to see an eruption or some other kind of volcanic activity when visiting the park.

The Hawai'i Volcanoes National Park is 335,259 acres in circumference and/or around 523 square miles from sea level to the summit of Mauna Loa. Hawai'i Volcanoes National Park has 150 miles of hiking trails to explore. Hike through rainforests, volcanic craters, and even hot deserts, all located in the Hawai'i Volcanoes National Park. Do not feel like hiking the whole time? Then take a drive through Kilauea, the world's only drive-thru volcano.

Active volcanoes are just one unique natural attraction that Hawai'i Volcanoes National Park has to offer visitors, but of course, the park is shaped by thousands and thousands of years of volcanic activity. For example, visit the Halema'uma'u Crater. This giant crater is full of steam vents that plume from the crater and local legend says that the Halema'uma'u Crater is the home of Pele, also known as the volcano goddess. The Halema'uma'u Crater has changed a lot over the past 10 to 15 years. For example, in 2008, the crater was completely filled with a lake of lava. But this lava disappeared in 2018! How did this happen? During the 2018 eruption, seismic activity caused the crater walls to fall into themselves which created a much larger crater. The result was that the crater went from around 70 to 78 million cubic yards in May of 2018 to the 1.2 billion cubic yards the crater is today.

Haleakala National Park—This park is located on the island of Maui; Haleakala means House of the Sun in the Hawaiian language. Haleakala is a truly impressive crater that towers over the entire island of Maui. It is so large, that you can see Haleakala from just about any point on the island. It stands at 10,023 feet above sea level and is in fact a dormant volcano. Haleakala is known for its unbelievable beautiful natural wonder with breathtaking landscapes and these views cannot be beaten.

The legend of Haleakala is centered around the demigod named Maui. Maui lassoed the sun while it was journeying across the sky. He was standing on the summit of the volcano, then used his lasso to slow the sun's movement, increasing the length of the day.

If you happen to be an early riser, there is no better place to view the sunrise than from the Haleakala Visitor Center. Each morning, visitors awaken early to drive to the visitor center to find a good spot to watch one of the most incredible sunrises on the planet. When the sun peaks on the horizon, the stunning swirling coloring almost dances through the sky and clouds. It is truly an incredible sight to behold. But if the idea of getting up before the sun is not the most appealing to you, no worries. The view from the visitor center is pretty spectacular during every part of the day and that includes a one-of-a-kind sunset that will also take your breath away.

Other attractions that pull hundreds of visitors to Haleakala National Park are the 30,000 acres of some of the most beautiful landscapes you have ever seen. With unique features like red sand and naturally occurring rock gardens and stunning waterfalls and streams, the beauty at the park can truly be overwhelming at times.

The beauty of Haleakala National Park can be explored through miles and miles of hiking trails that can also be accessed on horseback. While visiting, be on the lookout for some of Haleakala's wildlife and plant life. Haleakala National Park is known to be home to more endangered species than any other National Park in the country.

Hidden Gems
to Explore

Hawaii has dozens and dozens of beautiful beaches, tropical forests, mountains, volcanoes, waterfalls, craters, and other natural wonders. There are also some extremely popular activities that you can do while visiting the islands, including swimming, rock climbing, caving, scuba diving, surfing in a variety of ways, relaxing, shopping, sunbathing, hiking, horseback riding, exploring, etc. But there are some lesser-known things you can do and places to visit that you might have never of before, including:

Lanai Cat Sanctuary—do you love cats? Then the Cat Sanctuary on the island of Lanai is a must-stop for you. This sanctuary provides shelter and protection for more than 500 furry felines. These stray cats live and play in this 25,000-square-foot kitty paradise. The island of Lanai once had more stray cats than it could possibly hope to handle. The sanctuary was created to care for and protect these kitties from harm. Giving these cats a safe home not only benefits them but also helps to protect the wildlife of the island of Lanai. This shelter helps to prevent all of the cats from hunting rare birds and small animal species around the island. Plus, the male cats that are brought to the sanctuary are neutered to help with population control. And the best news for you is that this sanctuary is open to visitors who want to cuddle and play with more kitties than they have ever seen before. You can also volunteer and lend a hand and/or make a donation to support the cats' care and feeding. It is a feel-good experience all the way around!

Garden of the Gods on Lanai— Officially known as Keahiakawelo, the Garden of the Gods is made of natural rock formations. A little off the beaten path, the

Garden of the Gods is full of stunning red rock formations that you can explore and photograph. These rocks come in all different sizes and shapes; you will find large rock formations, boulders of different sizes, and small rocks along the ground. But be wary, because although it might be tempting to handle or remove some of the rocks it is not advised. Local legend says that messing with the rocks could bring the wrath of the ancient gods down upon you. As the legend goes, one day two wise men, one from the island of Molokai and one from the island of Lanai stood against each other in a challenge to see who could keep their fire burning the longest. The fiery landscape in the Garden of the Gods is a result of this great battle.

The Bamboo Forest— If you happen to find yourself on the island of Maui head over to the Bamboo Forest. The Bamboo Forest is a magical place that looks like it would be more at home in a fairy tale. You can find Maui's Bamboo Forest located along Pipiwai Trail in the Haleakala National Park. You will have to hike several miles to reach the Bamboo Forest, but the trip is well worth it. When you arrive, you will see the sunlight pouring through the massive bamboo stalks. Bamboo sways in the wind as birds sing and fly through the stunning towering trees. Be sure to wear comfortable walking or hiking shoes and do not forget the bug repellent. Plus, bring plenty of water and maybe a snack for the long hike to and from the Bamboo Forest.

Shopping

You cannot go to Hawaii and go home empty-handed, right? The Hawaiian Islands offer a large variety of shops, including small local stores with one-of-a-kind items only found in Hawaii, fun souvenirs and Hawaiian-themed storefronts, and more! Here are a few places you should check out if you find yourself in the vicinity:

Ala Moana Shopping Center is located in Honolulu. This happens to be the largest shopping mall in all of the Hawaiian Islands. In fact, the Ala Moana Shopping Center is the largest outdoor shopping center in the entire world! There are over 290 stores to explore and 70 different dining options in this shopping complex. With local treasures and boutiques and big-name brand stores, there is something for everyone at this shopping center. Additionally, the Ala Moana Shopping Center is known for both its massive food court with dozens of food options and its popular local sit-down restaurants like the Vintage Cave and The Pineapple Room. So, you will be able to refuel throughout the day as you are shopping.

Maui Swap Meet is located on the Island of Kahului. Every Saturday morning from the hours of 7:00 a.m. to 1:00 p.m., more than 200 local vendors come to the Maui Swap Meet to sell their goods. These goods include artwork, clothing, jewelry, souvenirs, local treasures, and much, much more! And do not forget about the amazing food vendors that are on site each Saturday.

Lahaina is located in Maui. This eccentric shopping area is one of the most popular shopping spots in Maui. The Front Street in Lahaina Town is loaded with some of the best shops the islands have to offer. These include fine art shops and decadent restaurants. Plus, there are some certifiably cool souvenir shops located in Lahaina as well. If you visit here be sure to stop by The Pearl Factory and the Maui Tees Outlet.

Coconut Marketplace is located on Kapa'a. This adorable and uniquely Hawaiian Marketplace cannot be skipped. The Coconut Marketplace is an open-air shopping experience and more closely resembles a little village than a mall. There is a wide array of stores and shopping experiences to be had at The Coconut Marketplace. The village is lined with galleries, small shops, boutiques, casual dining restaurants, and fun cafes. They have hula dancers for entertainment that takes place at 5:00 p.m. on Wednesday evenings and 1:00 p.m. every Saturday afternoon. Plus, there is even an impressive farmer's market on-site.

Kaup Store, which is located on the island of Maui has been a Hawaiian tradition since the year of 1925; the Kaup Store is exactly the type of store that comes to mind when you think about Hawaii. The Kaup Store is a Hawaiian-style country store where you can purchase Hawaiian snacks while shopping through the collection of fun antiques and household items.

WILDLIFE YOU MIGHT
SEE IN HAWAII

Hawaii is home to unique wildlife not seen in the rest of the United States. Many of these species are native to the islands and a good deal of the native wildlife is endangered. So, it is important that you do not disturb the wildlife or do anything to harm their natural habitat while visiting Hawaii. But the good news is you can still observe these animals and take all of the photos and videos that you would like!

So, during your visit, be on the lookout for these amazing Hawaiian creatures:

The Hawaiian Monk Seal— Also known as the Northern Elephant Seal, the Hawaiian Monk Seal is the official mammal of Hawaii and is the rarest species of seals on the planet. In fact, there are fewer than 100 Hawaiian Monk Seals left in the world, they are endemic to the Hawaiian Islands, and you can only find the remaining Monk Seals in Hawaii. If you do happen to see a Hawaiian Monk Seal sunbathing on the beach, be sure you observe it from afar. Do not try to approach the seal or disturb its peaceful rest. This is especially true if you see a seal pup; they are vulnerable and since mama seals come to shore to give birth, that pup might be extremely young.

Feral Wallabies— These cute little critters undoubtedly pose a major issue for the Hawaiian Islands. Feral Wallabies are an invasive species to the Hawaiian Islands and they have been causing damage to the fragile ecosystems on the islands. They were originally brought to the islands in the 1900s to be a zoo exhibit, but some escaped from the zoo and started breeding. They compete with other Hawaiian mammals for their food sources. But, if you happen to find yourself on Ohau, you might get a look at these mini kangaroos!

Feral Cattle, Pigs, Sheep, and Goats— Speaking of invasive species, beasts of burden and farm animals have been brought to the islands over the decades and now there are large amounts of feral cattle, pigs, sheep, goats, and even donkeys roaming around. These animals also compete for native animals' food sources, and they do breed fast. But remember if you see some of these animals wandering the islands to avoid them. These are technically wild animals and not the petting zoo-friendly farm creatures you are used to.

Hawksbill Sea Turtle— Sea turtles are a major draw to the Hawaiian Islands and the critically endangered Hawksbill Sea Turtle is one of the turtles people come to see. You will most likely spot a Hawksbill Sea Turtle swimming around the coral reefs, dining on sea sponges. These beautiful turtles have been hunted to near extinction because of their naturally decorative shells, which is one of the main reasons they find themselves on the critically endangered species list.

Nene— The official bird of Hawaii is also referred to as the Hawaiian Goose. The Nene is only located on the Hawaiian Islands of Maui, the Big Island, Molokai,

Oahu, and Kaua'i. You might see them flying to and from their nesting and feeding grounds. They love to dine on seeds, fruits, certain leaves, and flowers. They are now one of the rarest species of geese in the world because of overhunting by humans.

Dolphins— The warm tropical waters surrounding Hawaii are home to a large variety of marine life. One of the most well-known and beloved has to be the dolphins. Entire industries and businesses in Hawaii are centered around dolphin watching and swimming with dolphins. Dolphins are majestic marine mammals that attract tourists to the Hawaiian Islands in hopes of getting a glimpse of them.

Humpback Whales— Humpback Whales visit the Hawaiian Islands all the time and these marine mammals are a truly spectacular sight to see in real life. Probably the best time for seeing the Humpback Whales in Hawaii is during the months of December through April. These months are when large groups and pods of humpback whales migrate through the waters off Maui County. 10,000 Humpback whales will swim past the islands during these months. In fact, the official start of Humpback Whale migration season in Maui is on December 15th each year. This kicks off-peak whale watching season even though Humpback

Whales will start showing up as early as November and sometimes might be spotted in October or late September. The whales are migrating from their summer feeding grounds in the waters around Alaska.

Not all of the wildlife in Hawaii is cute and fun. While Hawaii is free from poisonous snakes, at least there are not any native poisonous snake species on the islands, and other large land predators, but there are still some extremely dangerous animals you should avoid at all costs. Most of these live in or around the ocean. So, be on the lookout for these dangerous creatures:

Long spined venomous sea urchins— These little critters may be small, but those tiny black spikes can pack a massive punch. Sea urchins will attach themselves to rocks and coral, and the danger to humans usually comes from when they accidentally step on one. The venom these sea urchins carry is not deadly to humans, but it is extremely painful and their spikes are known to break off and get stuck in the skin. To avoid getting injured by a sea urchin it is recommended to wear sea shoes while surfing or splashing around in the Pacific Ocean.

Boxed Jellyfish— The Boxed Jellyfish is arguably the most dangerous animal in or around the Hawaiian Islands. Sometimes known as the sea wasp or marine stinger, the Boxed Jellyfish packs a potentially lethal sting. These massive sea predators grow up to 10 feet long. The toxins in their sting will attack and target a person's nervous system, skin cells, and the heart. People who are stung by a Boxed Jellyfish could go into shock before they get out of the water, causing drowning, and other people may experience heart failure before they ever have a chance to seek help. Boxed Jellyfish are so dangerous that whole beaches will close down if they are spotted swimming in the area.

Tiger Sharks— While many species of sharks show little to no interest in people, the Tiger Shark is considered to be much more aggressive. In fact, they are one of the most feared sharks swimming around the Hawaiian Islands and in oceans across the world. Tiger Sharks can reach up to 13 feet in length and they have an amazing sense of sight and smell. While other species of shark are picky eaters that do not care for humans, Tiger Sharks are more open-minded. If another shark bites a human, it is usually because they mistook them for their prey and they swim off once they realize their mistake, Tiger Sharks not so much. Now, while Tiger Sharks may seem terrifying, and sure they are, they do not usually attack people and in Hawaii, there are typically two to three reported shark attacks each year and these attacks are rarely fatal. There have only been 11 shark-related fatalities in Hawaii in the last 100 years and considering the thousands of people who visit and swim around the Hawaiian Islands each year, these attack numbers are fairly low.

Cone Snails— Did you know Hawaii is home to 34 different cone snail species? This is one reason it is not a good idea to pick up random shells found on the beach or in the water. You never know what might be lurking inside. Cone snails are venomous and will not hesitate to lunge their head out of their shells and bite anyone who disturbs them. And yes, this venom can be extremely deadly to humans, depending on the type of cone snail that bites you. Many cone snails are not as dangerous and their bite may feel more like a bee sting, but other species pack a much deadlier punch. Some species pack enough venom in just one single bite to kill up to 10 people. So, do yourself a major favor and keep your hands off those shells.

Moray Eels— The Moray Eel is undoubtedly one of the most dangerous animals in Hawaii. With more than 80 different species, many of which can reach up to 13 feet in length, the Moray Eel is unfortunately extremely common in the waters around Hawaii. The good news is that Moray Eels do try to avoid people and they are more active after dark when most people are not swimming in the ocean. But an attack from one of these eels is extremely painful and they can do some real damage. They are aggressive if cornered or disturbed, so your best chance of avoiding running into one of these eels is to stay out of the ocean at night.

Great White Sharks— Movies like *JAWS* have turned the great white shark into an underwater villain, and they are terrifying if you come across them. They are the largest predatory fish on the planet and they have been known to grow up to 15 to 20 feet in length and can weigh around 5,000 pounds. And do not forget about those 300 razor-sharp teeth! So, yes, the great white shark is scary. But the good news is that while they are sometimes spotted swimming in the waters around Hawaii, they are not all that common. In other good news, the great white shark is not fond of eating people and if attacks do happen the shark quickly realizes its error and releases the person. But even these attacks are not a major concern in Hawaii because the great white is rare and encounters with humans are even rarer.

Yellow-Bellied Sea Snakes— While the Hawaiian Islands themselves are relatively snake-free, the ocean is another story. Yellow-Bellied Sea Snakes can stay submerged underwater for up to three hours and they are extremely venomous. They will often group together in large quantities and float on top of the water, waiting for the waves and current to sweep their prey by. While their venom is toxic to people, there have not been any reported fatalities from one of their bites in Hawaii and they go out of their way to avoid contact with people.

Brown Tree Snakes— Speaking of snakes and moving from the ocean to the land, the Brown Tree Snake, not native to Hawaii, is another invasive species. The Brown Tree Snake is native to Guam and Hawaiian officials have been working to cull their population on the islands as much as possible. They are venomous and aggressive towards people. So, avoid them at all costs, but it is unlikely that you will see one. Keep in mind that Hawaii does not have its own snakes so if you see a snake, assume it is a venomous Brown Tree Snake and back away.

Brown Recluse Spiders— Another land hazard is the Brown Recluse Spider, sometimes known as the Brown Violin Spider. These spiders are not aggressive and usually only bite when they get trapped against a person's body and another object, such as rolling over on one in your sleep or having one in your shirt when you put it on. They are not deadly spiders, but their bite can be extremely harmful to some people. They are recluses by nature and will hide from people and animals; they are also nocturnal as well. Many areas and states in the mainland United States are also home to the Brown Recluse.

While these creatures might sound scary, they should not keep you from planning your dream Hawaiian vacation. People are rarely harmed by Hawaii's wild or marine life. Just follow the safety instructions. Do not go into the ocean after dark; if they close a beach do not try to sneak in, do not stick your hand in strange holes, or dig around underwater rocks or coral, and wear your swim shoes. These precautions are more than enough to keep you as safe as possible when exploring the Hawaiian Islands and swimming in the Pacific Ocean.

CONCLUSION

Y ou would be hard-pressed to find a more beautiful place to take a vacation than the islands of Hawaii. With so many diverse habitats you could go from viewing snow-topped mountains to strolling through the desert on the same day. Home to the only tropical rain forests in the United States, you will have the ability to view and photograph some truly exotic wildlife not found anywhere else in the country. Swing by the Big Island to visit the Hawai'i Volcanoes National Park to view active volcanoes and relax on black sand beaches next to green sea turtles. Dine-in restaurants with some of the freshest ingredients you have ever had the opportunity to taste.

Try your hand at some of the more popular water sports that Hawaii has to offer. How many other places can you try to surf with so many different variations including body surfing, kite surfing, and windsurfing, and let us not forget about the traditional surfing method! Go snorkeling and observe coral reefs and the Hawaiian marine life. Scuba dive or swim with sharks if you are feeling more adventurous. Take a kayak and paddle through a tropical rainforest or hop on an inner tube and raft through a mountain stream.

Hawaii is truly a one-of-a-kind place to visit and the islands have more to do than you could possibly imagine. The key to a successful and satisfying Hawaiian vacation is to select the island that fits your personality and offers the most activities that fit your personal preferences.

References

10 Interesting facts about Hawaii. (2022). Hawaiian Airlines. Retrieved May 14, 2022, from https://www.hawaiianairlines.com/trip-planning-guide/10-interesting-facts-about-hawaii

21 Best State Parks in Hawaii. (2022, May 1). *Vacation Idea: Dream Vacation Magazine.* Retrieved May 14, 2022, from https://vacationidea.com/hawaii/best-hawaii-parks.html

25 Amazing Hidden Gems in Hawaii. (2022). *The Crazy Tourist.* Retrieved May 13, 2022, from https://www.thecrazytourist.com/25-amazing-hidden-gems-in-hawaii/

50 Fun Facts about the 50th State. (n.d.) Office of the Governor. Retrieved May 13, 2022, from https://governor.hawaii.gov/wp-content/uploads/2015/01/50-Fun-Facts-about-the-50th-State.pdf

82 facts about Hawaii (bet you never heard of Hawaii fact 32). (2019, September 9). Cosmopoliclan. Retrieved May 14, 2022, from https://cosmopoliclan.com/travel-with-kids/inspiration/facts-about-hawaii/

86 Fun & Unusual Things to Do in Oahu (Hawaii).
(2022, March 10). *Tour Scanner.* Retrieved May
15, 2022, from
https://tourscanner.com/blog/things-to-do-
in-oahu-hawaii/

Allen, Jordan. (2019, August 19). Why It's Illegal to
Take Sand from Some Beaches. *The Points Guy.*
Retrieved May 13, 2022, from
https://thepointsguy.com/news/why-taking-
sand-may-be-illegal/

Animals in Hawaii. (n.d.) A-Z Animals. Retrieved May
14, 2022, from https://a-z-
animals.com/animals/location/north-
america/united-states/hawaii/

The Atlas Obscura Guide To Hawaii: 64 Cool,
Hidden, and Unusual Things to Do in Hawaii.
(2022, March 23). Atlas Obscura. Retrieved
May 13, 2022, from
https://www.atlasobscura.com/things-to-
do/hawaii

Black Sand Beach at Punalu'u Beach. (2021). Kilauea
Hospitality Group. Retrieved May 13, 2022,
from https://volcano-
hawaii.com/attractions/black-sand-beach-at-
punaluu-beach-
park/#:~:text=Punalu%60u%20Beach%20Pa
rk%20is,the%20Hawaii%20Volcanoes%20Nat
ional%20Park.

Born of Fire, Born of the Sea. (n.d.). National Park
Service. Retrieved May 15, 2022, from
https://www.nps.gov/havo/index.htm?fbclid

=IwAR2GEon-
JfBz6qmVwihxAtFs7MawxgblkKCfM5Edwep
L96ncRZqoPxNbo0s

Cheung, M. (2021, July 29). 8 Unbelievable Gems in Hawaii You Might Not Know About. *Hawaii Travel with Kids*. Retrieved May 12, 2022, from https://hawaiitravelwithkids.com/unbelieveable-hidden-gems-in-hawaii/

Encyclopedia Britannica. (2022). Climate of Hawaii. In Encyclopædia Britannica Online. Retrieved May 14, 2022, from https://www.britannica.com/place/Hawaii-state/Climate

Fisher, Bruce. (2021). Top 5 Things NOT To Bring To Hawaii. *Hawaii Aloha Travel*. Retrieved May 14, 2022, from https://www.hawaii-aloha.com/blog/2015/10/16/top-5-things-not-to-bring-to-hawaii/

Fresh Bite Kauai. (n.d.) Fresh Bite Kauai. Retrieved May 15, 2022, from http://www.freshbitekauai.com/

Gallagher, K. (2019, November 11). The Best Bars and Clubs in Honolulu. TripSavvy. Retrieved May 13, 2022, from https://www.tripsavvy.com/the-best-bars-and-clubs-in-honolulu-4589338

Giovanni's Shrimp Truck. (n.d.) Giovanni's Shrimp Truck. Retrieved May 14, 2022, from http://www.giovannisshrimptruck.com/menu.php

Hanwell, C. The 9 Most Dangerous Animals in Hawaii. (2021, Jun 9). *Journeying the Globe.* Retrieved May 12, 2022, from https://www.jtgtravel.com/north-america/hawaii/most-dangerous-animals-in-hawaii/

Hawaii. (n.d.) National Park Service. Retrieved May 15, 2022, from https://www.nps.gov/state/hi/index.htm?fbclid=IwAR0AJ33hiQY8yMBT9km9nuKzPprUP_D2lNDDzwAc10RpQrRPscoETKrlJtY

Hawaii national parks LIST 2 national parks in Hawaii + 7 more national park sites. (2022). Flashpacking America. Retrieved May 13, 2022, from https://www.flashpackingamerica.com/hawaii-travel/national-parks-in-hawaii/?fbclid=IwAR3dRQeqyHn475dy_IN5Ue_YKUBN8nAH_3Xrdvbk8IclOnhtVMyk1Jv2odY#:~:text=There%20are%202%20national%20parks,2

Hawaiian Volcano Observatory. (n.d.) Active Volcanoes of Hawaii. United States Geological Survey. Retrieved May 13, 2022, from https://www.usgs.gov/observatories/hvo/active-volcanoes-hawaii#:~:text=Each%20island%20is%20made%20of,six%20active%20volcanoes%20in%20Hawaii.

Helena's Hawaiian Food. (2022). Helena's Hawaiian Food. Retrieved May 14, 2022, from

https://www.helenashawaiianfood.com/menu
pg.html

How Many Hawaiian Islands do you Know? (2022).
Skyline Hawaii. Retrieved May 13, 2022, from

https://www.skylinehawaii.com/blog/how-many-
hawaiian-islands-do-you-
know?fbclid=IwAR3wbeBOKhwqxugYAeU3
STanlVN2U0BuDubYxv9VepDfKkT4YUlS5
YlbQyg

Humpback Whales in Maui. (n.d.). Hawaiian Paddle
Sports - Maui Ocean Activities. Retrieved May
14, 2022, from
https://hawaiianpaddlesports.com/maui/hum
pback-
whales/#:~:text=During%20the%20winter%
20months%20of,in%20other%20species%20o
f%20whales.

In-Flight and Arrival Travel Requirements. (2022).
Hawaii Tourism Authority. Retrieved May 15,
2022, from
https://www.gohawaii.com/travel-
requirements

Information for Travelers Coming to the U.S.
Mainland from Hawaii. (2020, June 2). USDA
Animal and Plant Health Inspection Service.
Retrieved May 14, 2022, from
https://www.aphis.usda.gov/aphis/resources
/traveler/hawaii/hawaiian_products

Island of Hawaii Beaches. (2022). Hawaii Tourism
Authority. Retrieved May 15, 2022, from

https://www.gohawaii.com/islands/hawaii-big-island/things-to-do/beaches

Jurassic Valley Zipline. (2022). KUALOA RANCH. Retrieved May 14, 2022, from https://www.kualoa.com/jurassic-valley-zipline/

Kauai: The Garden Island. (2022). Hawaii Tourism Authority. Retrieved May 13, 2022, from https://www.gohawaii.com/islands/kauai

Kirk, K. (2016, August 4). The Best Places to Shop in Hawaii On Every Island. Tripping. Retrieved May 12, 2022, from https://www.tripping.com/explore/the-best-places-to-shop-in-hawaii-on-every-island?fbclid=IwAR28W20EUFnKzXCZX11Sew5Eb8w9SOttHdRF3reLJC7kiFeIGjRP8Ze6xDU

Klurman, M. (2021, August 14). 20 Reasons Maui Is the Best Hawaiian Island. *Reader's Digest.* Trusted Media Brands, Inc. Retrieved May 14, 2022, from https://www.rd.com/list/maui-hawaiian-island/

Leonard's Bakery. (2022). Leonard's Bakery Ltd. Retrieved May 14, 2022, from https://www.leonardshawaii.com/menu/wraps/

Miner, M. (2015, Sept. 8). 7 Things to Know About What You Can Bring Into and Take Out of Hawaii. *Hawaii Magazine.* Retrieved May 14, 2022, from https://www.hawaiimagazine.com/7-things-

to-know-about-what-you-can-bring-into-and-
take-out-of-hawaii/

Morton, M.C. (2014, August 15). Top 10 National and
State Parks in Hawaii. *The Guardian*. Guardian
News & Media Limited. Retrieved May 14,
2022, from
https://www.theguardian.com/travel/2014/a
ug/15/top-10-national-state-parks-hawaii

Na Pali Coast, Kauai: Heaven on Earth. (2022).
Hawaii. Retrieved May 14, 2022, from

https://www.hawaii.com/

Oahu. (2022). Hawaii.com Retrieved May 12, 2022,
from https://www.hawaii.com/oahu/

Oahu: The Heart of Hawaii. (2022). Hawaii Tourism
Authority. Retrieved May 13, 2022, from

https://www.gohawaii.com/islands/oahu

Opakapaka Grill and Bar. (2022). Opakapaka Grill
and Bar. Retrieved May 15, 2022, from
https://www.opakapakagrillandbar.com/

Paiva, Derek. (2015, November 10). Hawaii has 10 of
the World's 14 Climate Zones: An Explorer's
Guide to Each of Them. *Hawai'i Magazine*.
Retrieved May 15, 2022, from
https://www.hawaiimagazine.com/hawaii-
has-10-of-the-worlds-14-climate-zones-an-
explorers-guide-to-each-of-them/

Papahānaumokuākea Marine National Monument.
(2022, February 24). Office of National
Marine Sanctuaries National Oceanic and
Atmospheric Administration. Retrieved May

14, 2022, from
https://www.papahanaumokuakea.gov/

Pink's Hanalei. (2018). Garden Island Creations, LLC.
Retrieved May 15, 2022,
from https://www.pinkscreamerykauai.com/

A Rare and Sacred Landscape. (2022, April 27).
National Park Service. Retrieved May 14,
2022, from
https://www.nps.gov/hale/index.htm

Restaurants in Maui. (2022). *Tripadvisor.* Retrieved May
12, 2022, from
https://www.tripadvisor.com/Restaurants-
g29220-Maui_Hawaii.html

Sacred Cauldron: HAWAI'I VOLCANOES
NATIONAL PARK. (n.d.). National Park
Foundation. Retrieved May 12, 2022, from
https://www.nationalparks.org/connect/expl
ore-parks/hawaii-volcanoes-national-park

Shute, M. (2020, May 4). Most People Don't Know
These 10 Hidden Gems In Hawaii Even Exist.
Only in Your State. Leaf Group Lifestyle.
Retrieved May 13, 2022, from
https://www.onlyinyourstate.com/hawaii/hid
den-gems-hi/

Traveling and Shipping from the U.S, Mainland and
to Hawaii. (2022). State of Hawaii Department
of Agriculture. Retrieved May 15, 2022, from
https://hdoa.hawaii.gov/pi/pq/travel-
shipping-information/traveling-from-the-u-s-
mainland-to-hawai%CA%BBi/

Trucking Delicious. (2021). Trucking Delicious Kauai. Retrieved May 15, 2022, from https://truckingdeliciouskauai.com/

Turtles, Swimming, and Snorkeling at Punalu'u Black Sand Beach. (2022). Love Big Island. Retrieved May 14, 2022, from https://www.lovebigisland.com/big-island-beaches/punaluu/

What Animals Live in Hawaii? (2022). *World Atlas*. World Atlas. Retrieved May 12, 2022, from https://www.worldatlas.com/articles/what-animals-live-in-hawaii.html

Why Choose Kauai Over the Other Hawaiian Islands for Your Vacation? (2022). Koloa Landing Resort. Retrieved May 14, 2022, from https://koloalandingresort.com/why-choose-kauai-over-the-other-hawaiian-islands-for-your-vacation/

Wildlife. (2022). State of Hawaii Division of State Parks. Retrieved May 14, 2022, from https://dlnr.hawaii.gov/dsp/wildlife/

Your Name in Hawaiian. (n.d.) Retrieved May 14, 2022, from https://www.manasquanschools.org/cms/lib/NJ01000635/Centricity/Domain/171/Your_Name_in_Hawaiian.pdf

Made in United States
North Haven, CT
04 November 2022

26293341R00055